A

Thing

That

Is

D1262442

robert

lax

A

Thing

That

Is

edited by
Paul J. Spaeth

THE OVERLOOK PRESS
WOODSTOCK • NEW YORK

First published in the United States in 1997 by
The Overlook Press
Lewis Hollow Road
Woodstock, New York 12498

Copyright © 1997 Robert Lax

All Rights Reserved. No part of this publication may be reproduced or
transmitted in any form or by any means, electronic or mechanical,
including photocopy, recording, or any information storage and
retrieval system now known or to be invented without permission in
writing from the publisher, except by a reviewer who wishes to quote
brief passages in connection with a review written for
inclusion in a magazine, newspaper, or broadcast.

Library of Congress Cataloging-in-Publications Data

Lax, Robert
A thing that is : new poems / Robert Lax; edited by Paul J. Spaeth
p. cm.
I. Spaeth, Paul J. II. Title
PS3523.A972T48 1997 811'.54--dc20 96-29264

BOOK DESIGN AND FORMATTING BY BERNARD SCHLEIFER

ISBN 0-87951-699-2 (hc)
ISBN 0-87961-885-5 (pbk)

Manufactured in the United States of America

2 4 6 8 10 9 7 5 3 1

For

Emil
Antonucci,

whose

Journeyman
Press

be
gan

it

all

introduction

Lax remembers that when he was a child he once picked up a small flat stone and made a mark on it with another stone. After having done this, he placed the marked stone back on the ground with the idea that someone would find that stone and understand that another person had made the mark. This, he once told me, is the earliest remembrance he has of consciously creating a means of expression.

Years later, when his work *New Poems* (1962) was published, the first item in that collection began "one stone . . ." and calls to mind that childhood moment with lines like "i lift / one stone / and i am / thinking. . . ." *New Poems,* along with "Sea & Sky" (1965) and "Black & White" (1966), were early milestones in Lax's writing and were works that displayed the maturing of his style. The hallmarks of that style were simplicity, sometimes to the point of abstraction, and an imagery that was direct, personal, and natural.

The poetry of Robert Lax is a simple affair— simple and contemplative. When I say "simple" I mean it in a number of ways. Lax's poetry is simple because he uses few words to say much. Not only is there an economy of words, but many times the line itself is pared down to the point of containing one word, a part of a word, or even a single letter. The effect of this kind of display on the page is that the reader is forced to slow the pace of his reading and in so doing finds himself concentrating more than is usual on each phrase, word, syllable, and letter.

There is also a singleness in the image and idea being brought across in Lax's poems. The image and the meaning are not buried under the weight of excessive verbiage. Each word and each phrase can be viewed by itself. This directness is due in part to the fact that Lax seldom revises his poetry: the first draft is usually the last draft.

Finally there is a singleness of purpose, and that purpose is the poem itself. Lax doesn't write with an eye toward publication but rather writes for the sake of expression. The poem itself is the thing. If the poem is later published, then so much the better.

When I use the word "contemplative" in relation to Lax's poetry, I mean that it causes one to focus in a direct way on the image itself. Both the content of the poems and the visual display of the words on the page call the reader away from the rush of the world to a state of reflection. This reflection is directed toward people and objects, art and ideas, feelings and relationships.

"Spontaneous awe at the sacredness of life, of being," is one of the ways in which Thomas Merton defined "contemplation" *(New Seeds of Contemplation,* 1961, p. 1). Merton came to know well the life of contemplation and has become probably the most influential writer of his generation in articulating that life as it is lived in a monastic setting. Lax knew Merton before he entered the Trappists, while they were classmates at Columbia University. At a time when Merton was caught up in the idea of making a success of himself through building up his reputation as a writer, he characterized Lax's very different mindset in this way:

> His whole attitude about writing was purified of such stupidity, and was steeped in holiness, in charity, in disinterestedness.
>
> *The Seven Storey Mountain,* 1948, p. 236.

The disinterestedness that Merton speaks of can be likened to the indifference of the monk to the outside world or of the artist in the opinions of his critics. Later, Merton said of Lax, "He was born so much of a contemplative that he will probably never be able to find out how much" *(The Seven Storey Mountain,* p. 181).

When asked in an interview about the need for isolation in the life of a writer, Lax said,

> I think you really need to be alone during a good part of the day. . . . I think that the isolation itself brings things to the surface that otherwise just remain hidden. And that you get to know yourself as a writer by being alone quite a bit.   *New York Quarterly* 30, 1986, p. 20

All the numbered poems in this present collection were written from the early to mid-seventies while Lax was living for the most part on the Greek island of Kalymnos. Whereas Merton chose a Trappist monastery in which to work out his con-templative aspirations, Lax chose life on the islands of Greece.

Kalymnos is an island just off the Bodrum Peninsula of Turkey. It is one of the farthest-out of the Dodecanese Islands from the Greek mainland. Kalymnos is only twelve miles long and six miles wide and is beautifully mountainous. It is this Mediterranean setting that gave birth to these poems. In speaking of his life in Greece Lax has said,

I like being in a place where there is sea and
sky and mountains, trees, even olive trees,
and sheep and goats, shepherds. These are
things which are natural, sacral, ancient . . . .

New York Quarterly 30, 1986, p. 26

Something is always happening here that
gives clear, clean testimony to the human
quality of the person or people involved
in any action.

New York Quarterly 30, 1986, p. 28

The only poem in this collection not written in
Greece is the first unnumbered one, which acts as
an introduction to the rest. This poem Lax wrote
probably in the 1940s in his hometown of Olean
in the southern part of western New York. Olean
was a small town then and still is today. Lax's
desire for a simple and uncomplicated later life
was certainly influenced by his early life in this
town that lies nestled in the hills running along the
Allegheny River.

Like Merton, Lax did indeed leave the world
for a life of solitude. Much of his early life had
been spent in and around New York City. He had
held a great range of jobs, including work at *The
New Yorker, Time*, and *Jubilee*; teaching college
English classes; and even working in the script
department of a Hollywood studio. His experi-
ences with and love for circus life were turned into
a cycle of poems entitled *Circus of the Sun*

(1959) and were the basis for other material later collected in *Mogador's Book* (1992).

Where Lax differed from many other poets of his generation is that he didn't stay in this country, nor did he enter into academic life or join any literary circles. He left that behind when he began living in Greece in the early 1960s. Since that time, he has become perhaps better known in art circles than in strictly literary ones. Also he has become better known in Europe than in the United States and so in recent years has been published mainly in England and in bilingual editions in German-speaking countries.

The poems in this new collection have not appeared in print before. Within these pages you will find words of wisdom, humor, and philosophy along with contemplations of life and art, personal images, and images of nature. Perhaps the final word of introduction should be left to Lax himself in this excerpt from a letter to Susan Howe in 1975:

> the look of the poem: i've always
> liked the
> idea of a poem or a word as a single
> (arp-like image)
> alone on a page
>
> (an object of contemplation)

i like white space &
i like to see a vertical
column centered
sometimes verticality helps in
another way

image follows image
as frame follows frame
on a film

verticality helps the
poet withhold his
image until
(through earlier
  images) the
mind is prepared
for it.

Paul J. Spaeth
Curator of the Lax Archives
St. Bonaventure University

There is no poem, no painting
that will hold on paper or canvas
the look of the three trees
standing in the valley
with their young green leaves.

They are three girls
pouring speech like water
poised and waiting
for their dancing lesson.

They are three girls on tiptoe
with arms uplifted
dancing in the valley's early light.

A

Thing

That

Is

1

```
(to
e
rad
i                   drop
cate                ping

the                 deep
line
                    in
be                  to
tween
                    the         con
sleep               life        scious
ing                 death
                    con         un
&                   tin         con
wak                 u           scious
ing)                um
                                con
                                tin
                    whose       u
be                  oth         um
tween               er
liv                 name
ing
                    is
in
the                 be
womb                ing
of
night

&
be
ing
born

in
to
day
```

2

re this
move is
the this
line
of &
de that
mar is
cay that

be &
tween nev
er

work
work the
two

&
play &
play nev
play er

re the
move two
the
line this
is
of this
de
mar &
ca that
tion is
that

be
tween &
the nev
work er
year
the
(& two
va
ca the
tion) two

3

What
is
be
ing

what
is

ex
is
tence

can
the
rab
bit

be
said

to
be

if
it
is
dead

?

we
say
it

is
dead

what
is

is
that

?

4

a
thing
that
is

a
work
of
art

the
way
it
is

is
a
work
of
art

is
won
der
ful

it
is

a
thing
that
's
been
fixed

the
way
it
is

has
been
fixed

it
can
hard
ly
be

won
der
ful

which
is
bet
ter

to
be
here
now

or
to
be
there
then
?

----

the
on
ly
way
to
be

is
to
be
here
now

----

the
way
to
be
here
now

is
to
be
there
now

----

to
be
here
now

(there
is
no
there

there
is
no
then)

the
on
ly
way
to
be
(there
then)

is
to
be
here
now

----

the
way
to
be
there
now

is
to
be
here
now

the
on
ly
way
to
be

is
to
be
now

----

the
on
ly
there

there
is

is
here

----

here
on
this
spot

here
on
this
is
land

here
in
this
sea

here
on
this
earth

----

the
on
ly
place
to
be

is
to
be
here

----

but
here
has
broad

di
men
sions

here
&
now

----

here
in
this
sys
tem

here
in
this
un
i
verse

here
in
the
mind
of
God

----

all
heres
are
here

all
thens
are
now

25

6

my	
cat	nor
walks	way
a	&
cross	fin
the	land
ter	agree
race	to
	ex
chi	change
na	am
is	bas
rest	sa
less	dors
	&
she	walks
stops	a
&	long
licks	it
her	as
right	though
fore	it
paw	were
	a
trou	tight
ble	rope
in	
so	ri
mal	ot
i	quel
land	I'd
	in
leaps	buen
up	os
on	ai
the	res
par	
a	
pet	

7

if someone
were really
the last man
alive on
earth

he'd
not be
a hermit

he'd be
a sur-
vivor

& would
probably
feel called
upon

to father
forth a
new race
of men

or, at
least,
of beings

he might
(but maybe
  he would
  n't)

he might
for one thing,
not believe
he was the
last

or he might
be content
just to
watch the
days go
by

speculating
on what the
silence would
be like

when even
he had
vanished

8 | the
world
is
il
lu
sion

the
world
is
an
il
lu
sion

the
world
is
my
il
lu
sion

the
world
is
one
of
my
il
lu
sions

9

       everyone's a yogi now
& everyone's a zen buddhist
   everyone's a dope-fiend
    or an ex-dopefiend
      an alcoholic
    or an ex-alcoholic
  everyone's a homosexual
    or an ex-homosexual
& everyone's committed suicide at least once

where's there
left
to go

?

as far as arts are concerned
   everyone's a poet
   everyone's a painter
   everyone's a photographer.
almost everyone is a nuclear physicist, too

no reason to junk all this easily
acquired status: take it as the
status quo

& then ask
where do
we go

?

10 |

be
gin
by
be
ing

pa
tient

with
your
self

la
ter
you
can
be
pa
tient

with
oth
ers

(name
 of
 the
 game

 is
 pa
 tience)

i've
been   it's
liv   eas
ing   y
on
an   to
is   tell
land   him

in   what
some   's
one   hap
else   pen
's   ing

mind   he
            al
the   read
peo   y
ple
of   knows

the
island

are
the
ones

he
thinks

would
be
there

the
waves
be
have
the
way
he'd
ex
pect
them
to

12

to say that
i was in love
with any one
of them

would have been
kidding

to say that i even
lusted after any

would have been
an exaggeration

that i longed
for some sort
of relationship
is true

but what form
could it ever
have taken?

13

he
realized
quite
young

that
he
hated
people

&
would
like
to
see
the
world
laid
waste

a
little
later

it
came
to
him

that
if
he
followed
the
dark
thoughts
in
his
mind

they
could
only
lead
to
his
own
des
struction

he
de
cided
to
be
kind

to
translate
his
bad
thoughts
to
good

his
hate
to
love

he
suc
ceeded
quite
well

squirrels
ran
to
him
from
across
the
park
for
a
hand
ful
of
nuts

old
ladies
ap
proached
him
with

sweet
em
bar
rassed
smiles

con
fi
dent
of
his
kind
ness

the
closer
they
got

the
more
he
des
pised
them

the
more
he
des
pised
them

the
kind
er
he
be
came

the
kind
er
he
be
came

the
more
they
loved
him

the
more
they
loved
him

the
closer
they
came

don't
say
it
now

don't
tell
him
that

are
you
out
of
your
mind

watch
your
step
there

how
many
times
do
i
have
to
tell
you

if
you
say
that

she
thinks
this

do you know why
i think he left
me all that
money?

precisely so
i could worry
myself to death

not about the
money: about
life itself

i think he left
me in charge
of all that
leisure

so i could
think &
think &
think

& i think
he knew
it would
someday

drive me
mad

when i
was old
& full
of care

i met
one day
a lady
fair

a lady
fair
who said
to me

i come
to you
from off
the sea

i come
to you
from off
the sea

& wish
that you
would fol
low me

does
eve
ry
riv
er
run
to
the
sea

&
is
the
sea
a
home
for
me
?

the
sea
's
the
home
from
which
i
rose

&
home
ward
now
the
riv
er
goes

18

the   the
earth   sun
is   is
a   a
ball   bright

with   self
an   re
in   gen
ward   er
pull   ate

           light
if
it   if
was   it
n't   ev
          er
we'd   went
fall   out

(&   it
may   would
be   al
          ways
we   be
will)   night

the
sun
`s
first
ray

the
sun
`s
last
light

the
burst
of
day

the
fall
of
night

what's God
gonna do
this after

noon

?

unmoved
he'll move
something

every
thing,
really,

but in
a special
way

always the
same ways,

but always
with a dif
ference

some dif
ference

some where

wait till
you see

when
you
say
the   it
po   is
et   more
is   like
a   when
mak   a
er   man
        dies   Cre
you   a
should He   tor
not   goes
think   to
of   see
him   his

as   Mak
the   er
mak
er
of
a
mod
el

air
plane

22

each day
the same
walk up
the hill

same turns
same shad
ow of the
tree

each sta
tion of
the way

takes on
its own

set of
meanings

they &
went as
through near
lit ly
er as
a pos
ture si
      ble

&
      to
win know
now what
`d they
it were
a do
gain ing

for as
works they
      lived

that
would
help
peo
ple

live

live
long

for
one
thing

live
well

for
an
other

a place for
everything

& everything
in its place

a place for
the blessed

a place for
the damned

a place for
love

a place for
hate

(a place for
 stars

 a place for
 sun)

(a place for
 sand

 a place for
 trees)

a time for
everything

& everything
in its time

dream
black
black
coffee

in
small
gold
(em
 boss'd)
cup

cups
&
drinks

(brandy
 cognac
 b/b
 ?)

cock
tail
?

(side
 car)

a statue
smooth
rounded

of
don
q
&
sancho

or
other
rider
&
squire

(afoot)

chinese

smooth
quickly
carved

un
painted

more
a
ges
ture
than
a
fin
ish
'd
work

in
the
other
room

a
lady

(sculp
 tor

 don
 or
 ?)

big
hat

lady-face

smooth

smooth
as
statue

mask
like

china
doll-
like
face

sit
ting
at
low
coffee
table

flowers

other
(equally el
 egant - after
 noon-looking
 tea-time)
guests

coffee
&
drinks

in still
other
room

where
i
am

where

(when)

i
wake
up

the
day
the
world
end
ed

he
was
work
ing
on
a
pot

he
had
fin
ish
`d
the
pot

&
was
work
ing
on
the
han
dle

&
when
the
world
end
ed

he
had
al
most
fin
ish
`d
the
han
dle

(life)
is
not
hol
y

be
cause
it
is

beau
ti
ful

it
is
beau
ti
ful

be
cause
it
is

hol
y

the v's & w's in
the harbor

waves & wave
troughs

black wild waves
& yellow lights

nervous fretful
sea

unwilling to
talk

unwilling to
keep silent

waves pursued
by waves

glance back
over shoulder

restless sleepers
of the broad black
sea

all night they
talk

all night
they shout

calling hoarsely
one over the other

uttering their
manifold complaint

no one waits
answer

speaks & respeaks
the anguish of
his heart

quiet as a garden

evening on the island

in all the compounds

melancholy thinkers

eyes at a middle dis-
tance on the floor

no speech: lips
utter words

but heart

is silent

-----

antigone is
unappeased

the furies & every
vengeance still
pursues

electra mourns

cassandra pro
phecies

(times change, but
 ancient voices
 fill the air)

-----

blood guilt
is blood guilt

blood begets
blood

the gods are
unappeased

by human
justice

-----

all the ancient
battles

fought
refought

all the ancient
oracles

respoken

-----

impassive as
the statue's
brow

the melancholy
thinker's

lips speak
but are as
quiet as
stone

what says the
heart
the dark heart
darkly knows

what says the
sea

the black wave
tells the
sky

i won't believe
i'm really
alive

until i'm gladder
to be alive
here now
than to have
been alive
there then

living in greece
i may be
thinking
i am, was,
alive there
then

some byzantine
time
some classical
time

why think
that good?

i should
know better

i think good
any time except
the eighteenth
century

(not too bad)

the nineteenth
century

(bad enough)

or the twentieth

really, i'm
glad to be
alive in the
twentieth

not only glad
to be just
alive

but even to
be alive
just now
right now

yes, but i keep
remembering
a light in the
eyes of certain
figures in
frescoes

certain figures
in mosaics

that made
me wish
i was living
then

as though
living then

were to
live

forever

some life
some liveliness
in the eye
that seemed
eternal

eternally
alive
eternally
infinitely
joyous
& penetrating

(warm with
 the warmth
 of life
 exploding,
 even, with
 the joy
 of life)

yet there
forever

is it
that see
ing them
in some
mu
se
um

seeing
them still
preserved
still
living

made me
envy
their
state

?

not
sure

am
not
sure,
either,
that it
was envy
they gave
me, but
rather a
life

a spark
of living
to keep
alive

the
dance
of
the
waves

is
an
order-
`d
dance

the
dance
of
the
waves

is
a
solemn
dance

a
solemn
dance

an
order-
`d
dance

the
dance
of
the
waves

the
dance
of

the
waves

sol-
emn
dance

sol-
emn
dance

these   these
are   the
the   sounds
a-   of
wak-   waves
en-   a-   wak-
ing   wak-   en-
waves   en-   ing
              ing
these   waves
are   wak-
the   en-
a-   ing
wak-   waves
en
ing
waves

57

the
world
is
cov-
er-
'd

with
waves
of
wa-
ter

the
world
is
cov-
er-
'd

with
waves
of
light

waves
of
air

&

waves
of
wa-
ter

waves
of
light

&

waves
of
air

wings   drops
of   of
light   wa-
               ter
&
               sparks
wings   of
of   light
air

wings   wings
of   of
light   light

&   &

wIngs   wings
of   of
air   air

danc-   danc-
ers   ers

danc-   danc-
ers   ers

in   in
the   the
air   heav-
             en

danc-   danc-
ers   ers

danc-   danc-
ers   ers

in   in
the   the
heav-   air
ens

danc-
ers

danc-
ers

in
state-
ly

move-
ment

danc-
ers

danc-
ers

high

in
the
air

which started him dreaming of cities again; all the
cities in the south; all the cities in the west; tumbling
cities, rising cities; cities with their beggars; cities
with their crones

this one with the long robe, striding through the wind;
that one with the engineer's cap, and a smear of wine or
lipstick

the cities with their bays in sunlight

their ancient churches rippling on the water

what a beggar he had been in all those cities; what an
outcast; his cane tap-tapping in the quay; on all those
quays

beggar: one day happy, dancing in the sun; leading children
over the hill

night in the cold wind, wrapped in papers, moaning, and
the wineskin broken

----

the stir of the cities, the enormous rise of the
cities; no one made it, no one person made it; all
together they rose and stirred and made the city
rise

women from senegal wrapped and sheathed in silks
their turbans wobbling as they walked, their bracelets
jangling

arabs scuttling in the alleys

who was more the city than its most lost idiot?

the hawkers, the merchants; merchant-hawkers

the white-capped midget behind a mountain of candy

----

drunkenness of the cities
drunkenness in the early morning

fishermen seated among piles of shells;
white wine half-filling their glasses

----

could it be thus on every planet?

did every planet have its street of
assassins, its green-rug alley?

was it thus wherever a port had been
carved

wherever men went out to fish
or came into the city
to trade?

----

the sounds of the city, the noises,
the high-screaming sirens

shouts and buzzings, unpredictable
laughter

& a cry for help

----

crates of bottles unloaded
in the early
morning

----

they had all come down from the hills
& were in the city

they had all come in from the sea
& were in the bars

----

the city had no mind of its own;

swayed as the earth swayed,

turned as it turned

and those who lived
in the city followed
each other

each one with only
a tiny small light
of his own

they'd come to think
of pancho

as mrs pancho

& mrs pancho
as being the
dark abode
of heaven
& earth

they brought
all their problems
to her

& he resolved
them

----

the sea at night was seething
like a caldron

they didn't think of her
in their little bars

but she thought of them
& she thought of her
encroachments

she lay and tossed
in the harbor

& seethed as though
moved by fires

at the round
earth's center

----

boats called desperately
in the harbor

come to the edge of the
pier and catch my cable

lash me to the quayside
for i am sick of
travel

----

the night stood for miles and miles
above the city

there was no end to the night
above the city

----

the sea was having
one of her fits:

wanted to talk
& couldn't

wanted to talk,
and was talking

wanted to talk
was talking

but who could
hear her

who could under-
stand the words she
said?

----

the hills were
quiet

wind moved the
few trees

but the hills
were still

they kept as
still as they
could

to comfort
the sea

"great is the achievement
& fame of abundant rain"

rains, and doesn't wish
to rain

rains, & never thinks of
raining

rains & rains: abundant
rain

----

the sea is wild
in the harbor

an uprising
of waves

a clamor outside
the citadel

----

wind urges them

on

exhorts the waves

whispers a strong
& insidious rumor

----

the waves are wild
are frantic

desperate enough
to break through
their confines

desperate enough
to leap upon
the land

----

chaos
of
waves

chaos
of
waves

or
der
of
waves

or
der
of
waves

cha
os
of
storm

cha
os
of
storm

or
der
of
storm

or
der
of
storm

----

populations are the cities'
waves

populations are the cities'
storms

rising storms of the equinox

the rising storms
of fall

----

there was, after all, a
rhythm, and quite a
perceptible rhythm

to what the sea
said

one had to remark
the cadence

one had to make
note of where
the tone fell

then all of what
she was saying

became quite
clear

----

she was not
as wild as she
seemed

she was not
as mad

she had thought
for some time
before speaking
her mind

in this
manner

the voice of conscience is my mother's
voice. or when not hers, of one of my
sisters never my father's: he may have
given advice from time to time, but
not in the imperative mode.

my mother advised me not to do things
that were wicked. my sisters ad-
vised me not to do things that were
ridiculous. my father, when he advised
me, advised me against things that were
dangerous.

I remember his advise, of course, But my
mother's voice is not a matter of memory:
it is an ever-present often-admonishing
reality

I am making her sound far more of a
harping harpy than she was, or is. But
I am not talking of her manner, which
was sweet & controlled, but rather of
its secret, subterranean effect.

is there
a pre-
sence
in the
house

that
calls

?

a pre-
sence
in the
house

that
calls
us

chil-
dren

?

i
an-
swer

&
my
moth-
er

an-
swers

&
my
moth-
er's
moth-
er

an
swers

&
my
moth-
er's
moth-
er's
moth-
er

an-
swers:

what

?

what,
fa-
ther

?

&
my
fa-
ther

calls

my
fa-
ther's
fa-
ther

calls

my
fa-
ther's
fa-
ther's
fa-
ther's
fa-
ther

calls